Mauricette Vial-Andru

Let's Pray the
Rosary

Illustrations by Emmanuel Beaudesson

MAGNIFICAT · Ignatius

To my grandchildren

With thanks to:

Father Antoine-Marie Berthaud, O.P.,
and Father Didier Vernay, O.P.

Translated by Janet Chevrier

Illustration page 22 by Jean-Marie Michaud.
Illustration page 30 from Abbaye Sainte-Marie de Rieunette.

Under the direction of Romain Lizé, Vice President, Magnificat

Editor, Magnificat: Isabelle Galmiche
Editor, Ignatius: Vivian Dudro
Proofreader: Anne Dabb
Assistant to the Editor: Pascale van de Walle
Layout Designer: Elena Germain
Production: Thierry Dubus, Sabine Marioni

Original French edition: *Priez le chapelet mes enfants!*
© 2013 by Librairie Pierre Téqui, Paris
© 2015 by Magnificat, New York • Ignatius Press, San Francisco - All rights reserved.
ISBN Ignatius Press 978-1-62164-034-9 • ISBN Magnificat 978-1-941709-02-3
The trademark Magnificat depicted in this publication is used under License from and is the exclusive property of Magnificat Central Service Team, Inc., A Ministry to Catholic Women, and may not be used without its written consent.

Printed by DZS, Slovenia
Printed on February 2015
Job number MGN15003
Printed in compliance with the Consumer Protection Safety Act, 2008.

Between the author and the reader

"Do you pray the Rosary, as the Blessed Virgin so often requested?"

"No, that's only for old ladies."

"Not at all, many young people pray the Rosary."

"It's always the same prayer. I get bored and my mind wanders."

"But even when that happens, the Rosary lifts up your heart to Mary, who prays with you and for you."

"I'd rather pray to Jesus."

"Jesus came to us through Mary and still comes to us through the Rosary. Without Mary, we wouldn't have Jesus among us. The Rosary touches the heart of Mary. And she intercedes before God for you and your family. So, hang on tight to your rosary."

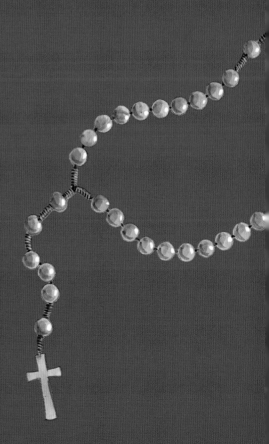

"The Rosary
is my favorite prayer."

Saint John Paul II

Contents

Praying the Rosary as a Family 6

Mary, Our Mother in Heaven 8

A Little History of the Rosary 10

Praying to Mary for Religious Freedom 12

The Prayer of the Chouans 14

The Saints and the Rosary 16

The "Living Rosary" of Pauline Jaricot 18

Fatima and the Prayer for Peace 20

The Rosary in Lourdes 22

Pompeii and the Apostle of the Rosary, Bartolo Longo 24

Many Ways to Pray the Rosary 26

What Joy to Say the Rosary! 28

Your Rosary and You 30

How to Pray the Rosary 32

Praying the Rosary as a Family

"Come on, children, it's prayer time."

Matilda, Helen, John, and Ann kneel down next to their mother before a statue of Our Lady of Lourdes. "Daddy, are you coming?"

"Of course, I'm on my way."

Daddy kneels down next to his wife and begins the Rosary: "In the name of the Father, and of the Son, and of the Holy Spirit." He says the first half of the Our Father.

Mommy and the children say the second half.

Mommy continues, "Hail Mary, full of grace. . ."

The children respond, "Holy Mary, Mother of God. . ."

The rosary beads slip through Mommy's fingers one by one as she leads each Hail Mary. The whole little family is deep in prayer.

But Ann, who is only four, begins to sway. The Rosary is a bit too long for her, so with a nod, Mommy lets her go off to play. John, who is six, valiantly sticks it out to the end. Fidgety Helen receives a nudge from her big sister and immediately settles down. As the eldest, Matilda needs to set a good example. Right to the end of the decade, she responds with a fine Hail Mary.

"Bedtime now, children."

This little family, who never misses a day without saying at least one decade of the Rosary, goes to bed calm and serene, to sleep in peace and trustfulness. This is a family that loves one another, in Jesus and Mary.

In each decade of the Rosary, you entrust to God all the events in your life—those in your family, your nation, your Church, and the entire world. You entrust your own personal experiences and those of your loved ones.

"The family that prays together, stays together," as Pope Pius XII once said.

Mary,
Our Mother in Heaven

It is hard to lose your mom at the age of nine. That is what happened to Catherine Labouré. Amid her tears, the little girl grasped in her hands the statue of the Virgin Mary that had pride of place on the mantelpiece at home.

"From now on, you'll be my mama," she whispered to her.

Yes, Mary is our Mother. Long ago, on the day of their baptism, many babies were entrusted to Mary by being presented on her altar. She is always close to us throughout our lives, especially whenever we are sick or sad.

One day, in the town of Pellevoisin, France, Estelle Faguette fell gravely ill. She was in despair, because her poor parents counted on her salary to make ends meet. So she wrote to the Virgin Mary, begging her to heal her, "O dear Mother, here I am, prostrate at your feet. . . Restore my poor body to health. See the sorrow of my parents. You know they have only me to support them."

The Blessed Virgin was touched by Estelle's letter. She cured her and appeared to her fifteen times, each time while Estelle was praying the Rosary.

All the saints have prayed to the Virgin. And Christians the world over continue praying to her today. Some wear her medal, others bear her name, some entrust their homes to her. Saint Bernard wrote her beautiful poems: each morning, he greeted her statue by singing the Hail, Holy Queen. One day, the statue leaned down toward him and answered: "Hail, Bernard." Imagine Bernard's joy!

Praying to Mary helps us on our way to heaven. The Holy Spirit is with her. When you pray to her in order to imitate her, the Holy Spirit will shower you with graces.

In the past, people wore garlands of roses on their heads in honor of Mary, and decorated her statue with them. These little headpieces were called "chaplets," from the word "chapel" (meaning "hat"). And so, a chaplet,* as rosary beads were once called, has its origins in these little garlands of roses in honor of Mary. The Rosary is like a crown of roses offered to Mary. Over time, Hail Marys took the place of roses. There are one hundred fifty of them in the original three chaplets of the Rosary, just as there are one hundred fifty psalms in the Bible.

*Chaplet: For Christians today, a Rosary is made up of 3 or 4 chaplets (see page 30).

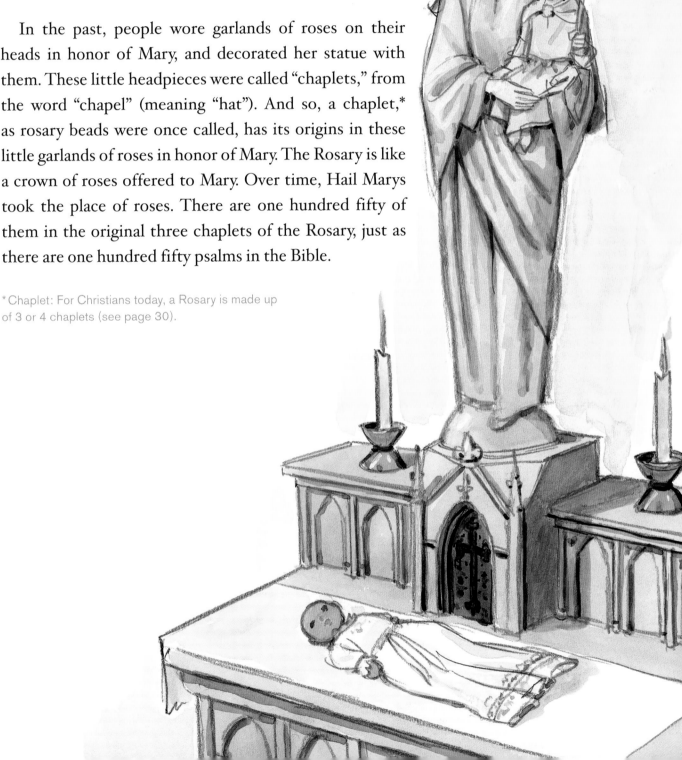

A Little History of the Rosary

In religious communities of the twelfth century, learned monks recited the psalms in Latin, the official language of the Church at that time. But in these communities, some of the brothers did not understand Latin, so they recited the Our Father and the Hail Mary with the aid of a *paternoster*, a knotted cord, the ancestor of today's Rosary beads. You might find it interesting to know that all religions use repeated phrases as an aid to prayer.

In the fifteenth century, a Dominican, Blessed Alan de la Roche, composed the Rosary prayer as we know it today. He arranged it so that everyone can contemplate the mysteries of the life of Christ (see page 30). That way everyone can memorize and meditate on the essential episodes in the Gospels. Thus, the Rosary is an aid to faith, like the sculptures and stained-glass windows of cathedrals that show scenes from the lives of Jesus and Mary.

Mary entrusted the task of preaching the Rosary to Brother Alan, and promised him:

"Have no fear. I am with you. I will assist you and all those who recite my Rosary. The Rosary will be a powerful weapon against damnation. It will destroy evil, deliver from sin, and expose heresy."

According to Blessed Alan, Mary first gave the Rosary to Saint Dominic.* When Saint Dominic evangelized the heretics** in the south of France, the people would not listen to him. They ridiculed him. They threatened him.

"This prayer is a weapon against enemies,
the sign of my love for Christians."
The Virgin Mary to Saint Dominic

Dominic was downhearted, so the Blessed Virgin appeared to him, "Dominic, my son, do not be surprised if you do not succeed. Urge the people to pray to me. Then you will harvest great fruits for the salvation of souls."

Dominic obeyed, and soon Hail Marys intermingled with Our Fathers were recited wherever the saint went.

At last, Dominic was heard.

From then on, Dominicans wore rosary beads on their belts.

*Saint Dominic (c. 1170–1221) founded the Order of Preachers, called Dominicans.
**Heretics are those whose religious beliefs are against those of the Church.
1585: Pope Sixtus V approved the use of the Rosary.

Praying to Mary
for Religious Freedom

In sixteenth-century Italy, the Turks massacred many Christians. Pope Pius V, who was a Dominican, took immediate action. He prayed the Rosary and asked all Christians to do the same. The Turks went on the attack. Christian ships gathered in the Mediterranean Sea and engaged the Turkish fleet near Lepanto,* off the coast of Greece. Badly outnumbered, the Christians prayed the Rosary and managed to win the battle. They freed fifteen thousand Christians who had been enslaved by the Turks.

The great victory at Lepanto saved Christianity. It was the first time a Christian fleet had succeeded in repulsing the Turkish navy—not through overwhelming force, but through the prayer of the Rosary. As an act of thanksgiving, Pope Saint Pius V instituted the annual Feast of Our Lady of the Rosary, celebrated every October 7. That is why the month of October is called the month of the Rosary.

Ever since that great Christian victory, the Blessed Virgin Mary is often seen holding rosary beads when she appears and asks that it be prayed.

Much later, other men would fight for religious freedom armed with the Rosary.

*October 7, 1571: Victory of the Christian Holy League at the Battle of Lepanto.

The Prayer of the Chouans

1793—in France, it was the Reign of Terror!* All of Brittany was up in arms. The countryside bustled with activity by night. Since the hoot of the barn owl ("chat-huant" in French) was a signal used by those who resisted the anti-Catholic government, they became known as the Chouans. The Chouans proclaimed:

"I'm fighting for God and my country."

"Glory to God! Long live the king!"

"Let's go to Mass and say the Rosary."

Protected by the people, priests who refused to submit to oppression continued their ministries in secret. Mass was celebrated deep in the woods, in barns, and even at sea. But religious persecution hardened. Priests were being guillotined every day. The Chouans, who fought to defend the Catholic religion, wore the scapular of the Sacred Heart and the Rosary on their chests. They were never without their rosary beads. They carried them into battle, in prayer and in song.

These valiant men fought to the death for their Catholic Faith. In 1801, Napoleon Bonaparte finally granted them religious freedom.

"At last," exclaimed White Wolf, one of the great Chouan leaders, "we've got what we wanted—through faithfulness to the Rosary."

The Rosary can change the fate of a nation. As you see, the Chouans preserved their religious freedom. But did you know that other countries have also been saved from brutal dictatorships** thanks to the Rosary? Here are some examples:

In Austria, in 1955, thousands of Austrians undertook to pray the Rosary every day, and defended Austrian independence against the threat of Soviet Russia.

In Brazil, in 1964, millions of women filled the streets of towns and villages reciting the Rosary. They too helped save their country from dictatorship.

In Chile, in 1973, one woman launched the Rosary Crusade. With the support of eight priests and two bishops, the country was freed from dictatorship in one year.

In 1986, the dictator Ferdinand Marcos peacefully left the Philippines after half a million people surrounded the leaders trying to reform the government and protected them from retaliation, armed only with their rosary beads.

*The Reign of Terror: following the French Revolution, a murderous regime that outlawed supporters of the king and the Church.

**Dictatorship: a tyrannical government that deprives the people of their liberty.

The Saints
and the Rosary

Even as a very young girl, Anne de Guigné liked to lead her playmates in processions to honor Mary.

"We'll place a little statue of Mary in a hole in an old tree in the park. Then, we'll take four big silk garlands I found in an old trunk, and we'll sing."

But Anne did not stop there. In October, the month dedicated to the Rosary, she gathered what she called "thornless" roses—which are sacrifices joyfully offered—and made them into a "bouquet" for the Blessed Virgin. She felt that Mary was truly our Mother. She would often take her rosary beads out of her pocket and fervently repeat: "Hail Mary, full of grace. . ."

One evening, she told a friend, "I said three Rosaries. Sometimes I got quite distracted, but as soon as I realized my mind was wandering, I refocused my attention."

Another child, a future saint, was just as devoted to Mary. Whenever the village church bell chimed the hour, Jean-Marie Vianney would make the Sign of the Cross and recite a Hail Mary. One day, his little sister, Marguerite, wanted to have his rosary, those precious beads that never left his side. John refused. His little sister screamed and screamed.

"Out of love for God, give it to her," his mother told him.

In tears, the little boy gave his rosary to his sister. How hard it was for him to part with it! But his mother, moved by the sight, took him by the hand, led him into the house, and gave him a little statue of the Blessed Virgin. The future saint, the Curé of Ars, never forgot the joy he felt on receiving this wonderful gift.

Along with his friends, Saint Dominic Savio founded the Company of the Immaculate Conception with one magnificent goal:

"We will do the will of the Blessed Virgin, and we'll teach others to pray the Rosary," he explained.

Pope Pius XI used to say, "Until the pope has said his Rosary, his day is not complete."

The "Living Rosary" of Pauline Jaricot

In Lyons, France, one Sunday in Lent, pretty Pauline, not quite seventeen years old, was at Mass. She was so moved by the priest's homily about vanity that she, so fashionable, so proud, decided she would dress like the poor. Among the workers of the neighborhood, she recruited other girls her own age to distribute her riches to the needy. She gave everything: clothing, money, food. Her startled parents tried to make her see reason.

So she started a collection for the poor: everyone had to give a few cents each week.

"But that's not enough," she thought. "I'll create a 'Living Rosary,' little groups of about fifteen people who will recite a decade of the Rosary every day. And it will be everyone's mission to recruit five other people to say the Rosary."

Pauline got her wish. The "Living Rosary" took off. It started in France, but soon spread to Switzerland, Belgium, England, America, Canada, Colombia, and even to Africa.

"Here's the idea," Pauline explained to her supporters, "I'll buy a place on the hillside of Fourvière, a hill in the town of Lyons, to house the Association of the Living Rosary. It will be a place of prayer dedicated to Our Lady of Loreto."

"Very good," said one of the organizers going even one better, "and we will send books, holy icons, medals, and above all, rosaries to anyone who asks!"

1826: Pauline Jaricot founded the Association of the Living Rosary.

Pope Gregory XVI granted approval to the "Living Rosary." Pauline had succeeded. Around 1832, the "Living Rosary" numbered a million members.

Early in the morning of January 9, 1862, Pauline murmured, "Mary, O Mary, I am entirely yours. . ."

With that, she left this life in the light of God.

Her funeral was that of a poor woman, but she was rich in what really matters: she had spread the faith through the "Living Rosary."

Fatima and the Prayer for Peace

One fine spring morning, May 13, 1917,* in the little village of Fatima, Portugal, seven-year-old Jacinta and her nine-year-old brother, Francisco, went with their cousin Lucia to tend the sheep. The children did not forget to say the Rosary before they began playing as they watched over the flock.

Suddenly, a brilliant light surrounded them. Above a little oak tree, a young woman dressed in white stood smiling at them. She was holding a rosary. The children were frightened.

"Where are you from?" asked Lucia.

"I'm from heaven."

"What do you want of us?"

"I have come to ask you to return here six times, at the same hour on the thirteenth of every month. Recite the Rosary every day for peace in the world and an end to the war."**

Jacinta told her parents everything that had happened. A beautiful lady had asked for the Rosary to be prayed to gain peace.

*May 13, 1917: The first apparition of the Blessed Virgin appeared to the three visionaries of Fatima.

**The First World War: From 1914 to 1918, the entire world was at war.

On June 13, around fifty people gathered to see the apparition.
"What do you wish of me?" Lucia asked the Lady when she appeared.

"I wish you to come on the thirteenth next month, that you say the Rosary every day, and that you learn to read." Almost four thousand people turned out to see the apparition on July 13. The Lady insisted on the daily Rosary.

"I wish you to continue saying the Rosary every day in honor of Our Lady of the Rosary, to obtain peace in the world and an end to the war."

Then she showed the children the hell to which unrepentant sinners go.

On October 13, 1917, more than fifty thousand people were present at the final apparition, when the Lady said:

"I am Our Lady of the Rosary. I wish that the Rosary continue to be prayed every day. I desire a chapel be built in this place in my honor."

Suddenly, the sun began spinning, shooting out rays of every color. At one point, it seemed to plummet down upon the crowd. Some screamed it was the end of the world. Others, who had come to mock, begged forgiveness. Fatima became a center of pilgrimage.

The Rosary in Lourdes

On February 11, 1858,* in the town of Lourdes, France, Bernadette was on her way to the Massabielle grotto to gather firewood with her sister and her little neighbor Jeanne. The grotto was before them, but a little stream blocked the way. Her sister Toinette and Jeanne took off their clogs and started wading across. But Bernadette hesitated and remained alone. Hearing something like a gust of wind, she looked up. In the grotto, she saw a lady dressed in white. Stunned, the little girl reached into her pocket, took out her rosary beads, and tried to make the Sign of the Cross. But her hand seemed frozen. She could not raise it to her forehead.

The lady, who had a rosary on her arm, took it in her hands and made the Sign of the Cross. With that, Bernadette did the same—she could move her hand again! Falling to her knees, she recited the Rosary. When Bernadette had finished, the beautiful lady gestured for her to come near. But Bernadette did not dare, and the vision disappeared.

Two days later, Bernadette returned to the grotto with some friends.

"If it's the devil, we'll chase him away with some holy water," they said.

The little group knelt down in front of the grotto and took their rosaries out of their pockets. Bernadette had not finished the first decade when she cried out:

"She's there! She's smiling."

22

It was during the third apparition that the lady asked Bernadette to come to the grotto for fifteen days. Bernadette obeyed. Each time she went to the grotto, she knelt down and began the Rosary.

"Pray for sinners," the lady told her, but still Bernadette did not know her name.

During the eighth apparition, the Virgin instructed Bernadette to convey her message:

"Repentance, repentance, repentance."

Then, one day, she revealed to her:

"I am the Immaculate Conception."**

Since then, Lourdes has become the greatest pilgrimage site in the world, and the Rosary is prayed by millions of pilgrims in front of the Grotto of the Apparitions.

Our Lady Immaculately Conceived is the patroness of the United States, and the Solemnity of the Immaculate Conception, December 8, is a holy day of obligation for American Catholics.

*1858: The first apparition of the Blessed Virgin appeared to Bernadette.

**Immaculate Conception: a title for the Virgin Mary, free from all sin from the moment of her conception.

Pompeii and the Apostle of the Rosary, Bartolo Longo

Born in 1841 in Italy, Bartolo Longo was a lawyer. He was interested in the spirit world and in trying to contact the dead (this kind of activity is forbidden by the Church). One day, struck by a feeling of total despair, he heard a call in his heart: "He who spreads the Rosary is saved!"

With that, he renounced his sinful behavior, repented, and became a Third Order Dominican. He then decided to build a sanctuary in Pompeii, dedicated to the Virgin of the Holy Rosary.

Pompeii is the ancient city which, in A.D. 79, when it had hardly been Christianized, was buried by an eruption of Mount Vesuvius. The volcano exploded so suddenly, the people were surprised in their beds and trapped under the burning ash gushing from the crater. Pompeii was forgotten for centuries until archeologists began excavations there, and the whole world learned of the tragic fate of the town's poor inhabitants.

At the sanctuary Bartolo founded, the community of the Daughters of the Holy Rosary quickly grew. But Bartolo did not stop there. One charitable project followed another in aid of the poor and the children of prisoners. He wrote books and prayers. In his writings, he recommended the contemplation of the mysteries of the life of Jesus. Leo XIII, the Pope of the Rosary, supported and encouraged him.

Bartolo Longo spoke of the Rosary as a sweet chain linking us to God, a link of love that unites us to the angels.

In Belgium, the Rosary is prayed in the town of Beauraing to Mary, "the Virgin of the heart of gold," and in Banneux, to Mary, "the Virgin of the poor." In Czestochowa, Poland, a miraculous wooden icon of Mary is venerated by the praying of the Rosary. In Loreto, Italy, where Mary's house was miraculously transported, the Rosary is fervently prayed. It is also prayed in Guadalupe, Mexico, where Mary, the patron of the Americas, appeared to Saint Juan Diego, a poor native.

"The Rosary is a treasure of graces."
Pope Paul VI

1980: the beatification of Bartolo Longo.

Many Ways to Pray the Rosary

The Rosary is said with the aid of beads attached at regular intervals along a little chain or cord. But as you will see, the beads can take many different forms.

Have you ever heard of Brother Marcel Van? He was born in Vietnam in 1928 and died in a concentration camp in 1959 at the age of thirty-one. He was persecuted for his Catholic Faith.

Marcel Van was devoted to the Blessed Virgin, and he loved to recite the Rosary in her honor. One day, when he was only seven, a heartless school teacher decided to put a stop to his prayers and took away his beads. But the little boy remained faithful to Mary. Instead, he used ten black beans, moving them from one pocket to another in order to keep track of his prayers. But the cruel schoolmaster spotted him and took away the beans. So Marcel then made ten knots in the cord he used as a belt. But the master was furious upon discovering his ploy.

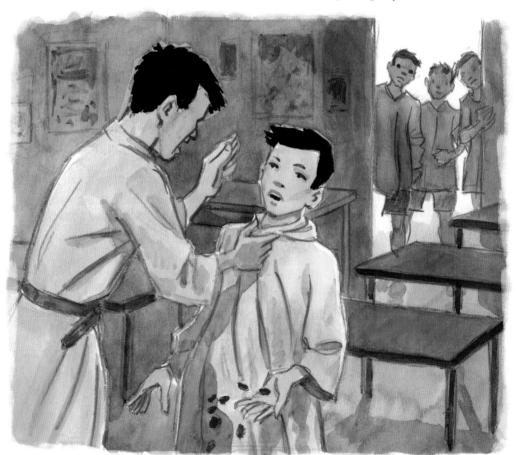

"What!? Still praying to your Blessed Virgin?"

He struck Marcel three times. But the little boy didn't say a word. He went on praying the Rosary by counting on his ten fingers!

"This way I can say my Rosary without anyone noticing. Even if it costs me my ten fingertips, I'll never stop expressing my love for Mary through the Rosary! It's thanks to the Rosary that Mother Mary has always come to my assistance."

"Children must be accustomed to reciting the Rosary. Lay the Rosary by the ear of the ailing, that he may repent and have a peaceful death."
The Blessed Virgin to Saint Angela in 1535

What Joy to Say the Rosary!

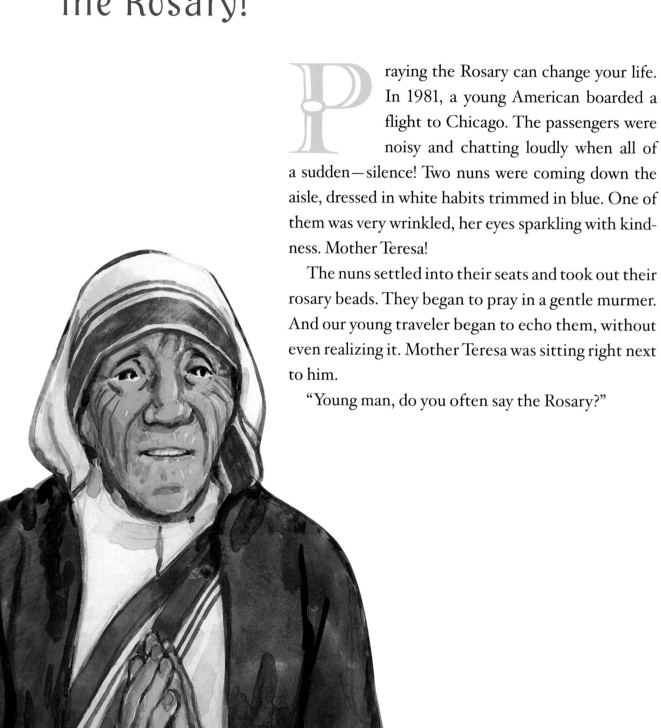

Praying the Rosary can change your life. In 1981, a young American boarded a flight to Chicago. The passengers were noisy and chatting loudly when all of a sudden—silence! Two nuns were coming down the aisle, dressed in white habits trimmed in blue. One of them was very wrinkled, her eyes sparkling with kindness. Mother Teresa!

The nuns settled into their seats and took out their rosary beads. They began to pray in a gentle murmer. And our young traveler began to echo them, without even realizing it. Mother Teresa was sitting right next to him.

"Young man, do you often say the Rosary?"

"No, not really."

So, with a smile, the nun laid her beads in the young man's hands and said, "Well, you will now!"

When he tells this story, this young American admits that, from that day on, his life was changed. He understood that what really counts is not money, or titles, or possessions. It is the love we have for others, the love that Mother Teresa showed him that day by encouraging him to pray the Rosary.

"After the holy Sacrifice of the Mass, the Rosary is the most divine of prayers."
Saint Charles Borromeo,
16th century

29

Your Rosary and You

To pray the Rosary is to contemplate along with Mary the life of Jesus. The repeated words are an aid to your prayer. Each event in the life of Jesus is a mystery.* With each decade (each set of ten Hail Marys) of a Rosary, we meditate** upon one mystery. There are twenty decades. You can say the complete Rosary, all twenty decades, if you wish. Or you can say one set of five mysteries (see list page 32).

You can also recite just one decade, at any time of day, anywhere you are—in your bedroom, on the bus, on a train, or, like Mother Teresa, on a plane. And not just during the school year, but on vacation, too. The main thing is your desire to know Mary and Jesus better and to imitate them.

You should recite the prayers slowly and patiently. Every Our Father and every Hail Mary is like a rosebud of thanksgiving to the glory of the Father, the Son, and the Holy Spirit. Think about how Jesus came into this world, offered his life, and rose again so that you might join him in heaven.

Today, there are classes to teach children how to pray the Rosary. Father Anthony, for instance, an instructor of the Rosary, visits classrooms to explain the history of the Rosary and its beauty. At the end of the class, the students and their teacher draw a number from one to twenty out of a hat; each number corresponds to a mystery in the Rosary. That evening, at home, each prays ten Hail Marys while contemplating the mystery he picked.

In this way, the prayers of the entire class make up at least one whole Rosary. What a beautiful bouquet of roses to offer up to the Virgin, roses directly from the heart of each person that touch the heart of our Mother Mary! Everyone can pray a decade—it doesn't take longer than brushing your teeth!

*Mystery: an episode from the life of Jesus and Mary, whose contemplation is an infinite source of treasure.
**To meditate: to think about Jesus and Mary with love and wonderment as guides for our lives.

How to Pray the Rosary

The Rosary is made up of three or four chaplets. All together, the original three (the Joyful, Sorrowful, and Glorious Mysteries) equate with the one hundred fifty psalms in the Bible. The fourth chaplet, the Luminous Mysteries, was added by Saint John Paul II. Each chaplet contains five mysteries.

Each mystery is prayed by a decade, or ten Hail Marys, preceded by one Our Father and concluded with one Glory Be. To start your chaplet, you say the Apostles' Creed followed by three Hail Marys (often offered for the pope's intentions or to grow in faith, hope and love) and a Glory Be.

The Joyful Mysteries:

The Annunciation
The Visitation
The Nativity
The Presentation in the Temple
The Finding of the Child Jesus

The Sorrowful Mysteries:

The Agony in the Garden
The Scourging at the Pillar
The Crowning with Thorns
The Carrying of the Cross
The Crucifixion

The Luminous Mysteries:

The Baptism of the Lord
The Wedding at Cana
The Proclamation of the Kingdom
The Transfiguration of the Lord
The Institution of the Eucharist

The Glorious Mysteries:

The Resurrection
The Ascension
The Descent of the Holy Spirit
The Assumption of Mary
The Coronation of Mary

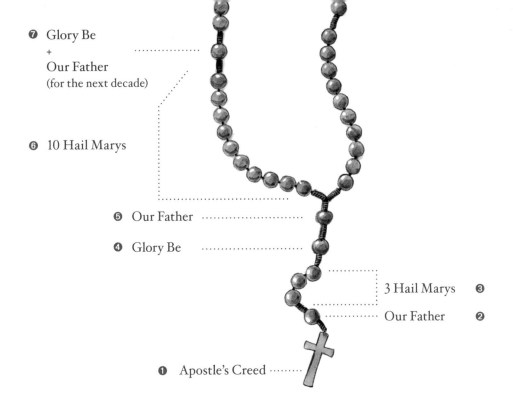

❼ Glory Be
+
Our Father
(for the next decade)

❻ 10 Hail Marys

❺ Our Father

❹ Glory Be

3 Hail Marys ❸

Our Father ❷

❶ Apostle's Creed

The Apostles' Creed

I believe in God,
the Father almighty,
Creator of heaven and earth,
and in Jesus Christ, his only Son, our Lord,
who was conceived by the Holy Spirit,
born of the Virgin Mary,
suffered under Pontius Pilate,
was crucified, died and was buried;
he descended into hell;
on the third day he rose again from the dead;
he ascended into heaven,
and is seated at the right hand of God
  the Father almighty;
from there he will come to judge the living
  and the dead.
I believe in the Holy Spirit,
the holy catholic Church,
the communion of saints,
the forgiveness of sins,
the resurrection of the body,
and life everlasting.
Amen.

The Our Father

Our Father, who art in heaven,
hallowed be thy name;
thy kingdom come;
thy will be done on earth
as it is in heaven.
Give us this day our daily bread;
and forgive us our trespasses
as we forgive those who
  trespass against us;
and lead us not into temptation,
but deliver us from evil.
Amen.

The Hail Mary

Hail Mary, full of grace,
the Lord is with thee,
blessed art thou among
  women
and blessed is the fruit
  of thy womb, Jesus.
Holy Mary, Mother of God,
pray for us sinners now
and at the hour of our death.
Amen.

The Glory Be

Glory be to the Father,
and to the Son,
and to the Holy Spirit.
As it was in the beginning,
is now, and ever shall be,
world without end.
Amen.

You may add after each Glory Be:
"Oh my Jesus, forgive us our sins.
Save us from the fires of hell.
Lead all souls to heaven,
especially those in most need
  of thy mercy."